Peoples of the Mountains

Robert Low

FRANKLIN WATTS

NEW YORK•LONDON•SYDNEY

This edition first published in the UK in 1997 by
Franklin Watts
96 Leonard Street
London
EC2A 4RH

© 1996 The Rosen Publishing Group, Inc., New York

Picture credits: Cover and p. 4 © P. Bernard/ANAKO Editions; p. 7 © ANAKO Editions;
p. 8 © Mimi Cotter/International Stock; p. 11 © M. Huteau/ANAKO Editions; pp. 12,
19 © H. Lam Duc/ANAKO Editions; p. 15 © D. P. Valentin/ ANAKO Editions;
p. 16 © Al Clayton/International Stock; p. 20 © C. Michel/ ANAKO Editions.

A CIP catalogue record for this book is available from the British Library.

ISBN 0 7496 2868 5

Printed in the United States of America

Contents

What is a mountain?

A mountain is like a very, very big hill. Several mountains side by side are called a mountain range.

In between mountains there are valleys. These can be wide and flat, or narrow with steep sides.

It is often cold and windy at the top of mountains. Some mountains are so high their tops are always covered in snow.

◄ The fields and trees on these mountains in China show that the climate here is quite warm.

Peoples of the mountains

The world's mountain ranges are home to many peoples.

The **Ladakhi** live in the **Himalayas** in Asia. In the summer it is very hot during the day, but freezing at night. The **Miao** also live in mountains in Asia, mostly in China.

The **Aymara** live in the **Andes** in South America. The weather in the Andes and in the mountains in China is not as harsh as it is in the Himalayas.

The Ladakhi people live in the Himalayas ▶
where winters are very cold.

Plants and animals

Plants must be tough to survive the harsh climate of the Himalayas. Where the Miao live, the climate in the mountains is warmer. Many plants and trees grow there.

Most mountain animals have thick fur to keep them warm. **Yaks**, bears and sheep live in the Himalayas.

Llamas, **alpacas** and chinchillas live high in the Andes.

◄ Alpacas are a type of small llama. They have long, soft wool.

Getting about

Getting about in mountains is difficult. Mountain passes, where the land is a little lower and less steep, are the best routes.

To cross narrow valleys, the Ladakhi build hanging bridges of honeysuckle vines. The Miao cross rivers on long, flat boats.

There are many lakes and rivers in the Andes. The Aymara cross them on boats and large rafts they make from bundles of reeds.

The Miao use long bamboo poles to push and ▶ steer their boats through the water.

Fishing and farming

Only tough crops can grow in the rocky soil and cold climate of the Himalayas and Andes. The Aymara and the Ladakhi grow potatoes and barley. Because their mountains are warmer, the Miao can grow crops such as rice, beans, peanuts and cotton.

The Aymara fish in lakes and rivers and keep llamas and alpacas. The Ladakhi have yaks, sheep, goats and cattle, which graze in nearby valleys. The Miao keep pigs and breed fish in the fields where the rice is grown.

◀ Ladakhi children help look after the family's animals.

Food

The Ladakhi eat mostly meat, bread and butter and cheese made from yak milk. They drink green tea with butter and salt. Butter stops their lips getting chapped in the cold.

The Aymara eat meat, fish and the food they grow on their farms.

The Miao eat pork, rice and pickled vegetables, like peppers and cucumbers. Families store food for the winter by keeping it in a mixture of salt and water.

The Miao often cook meat in shallow pans ▶
over open fires.

14

Clothes

The Andes and Himalayas are cold, so the Aymara and Ladakhi need to wear really warm clothes for most of the year. The Aymara make theirs from wool they get from their alpacas. The Ladakhi wear clothes made from the wool of their sheep.

The Miao live in a milder area, so do not need such warm clothes. They embroider beautiful patterns on their cotton clothes. Many of the patterns tell stories.

◀ The Aymara make their clothes from alpaca wool, often dyeing it brilliant colours.

Homes

Harsh mountain climates mean that houses there must be strong. The Aymara build one-room homes from **turf**. The roofs are **thatched**.

The Ladakhi use stones and mud bricks to build two-storey homes with thick walls. The roofs are made of wooden poles and tree branches held down with mud.

The Miao build wooden houses on stilts on the sides of the mountains.

Most Ladakhi houses have walls a metre thick. ▶
This helps to keep them warm.

Family and community

Ladakhi families live together in villages. Families help each other. Ladakhi boys take care of the family's herds. Girls help out at home and in the fields. Today, many Ladakhi people work in nearby towns to earn money for their families.

The Miao also live in villages made up of several families. Now many young Miao are leaving their villages for life in the cities of Asia.

◀ A festival is a chance for these Miao girls to wear their beautiful traditional clothes.

Changing times

Many mountain peoples no longer live
in the same way as their **ancestors**.
The world around them is changing.
Television has reached the mountain
villages of the Miao. Many Ladakhi have
left the Himalayas to work in cities.
And Aymara men now work in mines or
factories in nearby towns or cities.

These changes make many of the mountain
peoples sad. But they are still proud of their
history and their traditional ways.

Glossary

alpaca	Type of llama that has long, fine wool.
ancestor	Relative who lived before you did.
Andes	Mountain range in South America.
Aymara	A people who live in the Andes.
Himalayas	Mountain range in Asia, north of India.
Ladakhi	A people who live in the Himalayas.
Miao	A people who live in mountains in Asia, mainly in China.
thatch	Grass or leaves tightly woven together to make a roof.
turf	Thick blocks of grass and the earth beneath which can be used to build walls.
yak	A long-haired type of ox that lives only in the Himalayas.

Index